Marketing Your Small Business Online in 2025

Terry C Power

Table of Content:

- ❖ Emerging Trends and Technologies
- ❖ Creating a Sustainable Marketing Plan

Introduction

In the rapidly evolving digital landscape, marketing your small business online in 2025 requires a blend of time-tested strategies and cutting-edge innovations. The internet has transformed how businesses reach and engage with their customers, offering unprecedented opportunities for growth and visibility. However, with these opportunities come challenges that can be daunting for small business owners who must navigate a complex and ever-changing environment.

This book, "Marketing Your Small Business Online in 2025," is designed to be your comprehensive guide through this intricate landscape. Whether you're a seasoned entrepreneur looking to refine your strategies or a newcomer eager to make your mark, this book will equip you with the knowledge and tools necessary to succeed in the digital age.

The New Age of Online Marketing

The year 2025 marks a significant era in online marketing, characterized by advanced technologies, increased consumer expectations, and the growing importance of data-driven decision-making. As artificial intelligence (AI), machine learning, and automation become more integrated into marketing strategies, small businesses must stay ahead of these trends to remain competitive.

Understanding the Modern Consumer

Today's consumers are more informed and discerning than ever before. They demand personalized experiences, swift responses, and seamless interactions across various platforms. Understanding their behaviors, preferences, and pain points is crucial for crafting effective marketing campaigns. This book will delve into the techniques for gathering and analyzing customer data, creating buyer personas, and tailoring your messaging to resonate with your target audience.

Building a Robust Online Presence

Your online presence is the foundation of your digital marketing efforts. It encompasses your website, social media profiles, online reviews, and more. In this book, you'll learn how to create a professional and engaging website, optimize it for search engines, and maintain a cohesive brand identity across all online channels. We'll also explore the importance of user experience (UX) design and how it can significantly impact your conversion rates.

Content Marketing: The Heart of Digital Strategy

Content remains king in the realm of digital marketing. High-quality, relevant content attracts, engages, and retains customers. From blog posts and articles to videos and infographics, this book will provide you with actionable tips for developing a content marketing strategy that drives traffic and builds trust with your audience. You'll discover the secrets to crafting compelling stories, utilizing various content formats, and leveraging content distribution channels effectively.

Mastering SEO and Social Media

Search engine optimization (SEO) is essential for improving

your online visibility and driving organic traffic to your website. We'll guide you through the latest SEO techniques, from keyword research and on-page optimization to link building and technical SEO. Additionally, social media marketing plays a pivotal role in connecting with your audience on a personal level. This book will help you navigate the ever-changing social media landscape, choose the right platforms, and create engaging content that fosters community and brand loyalty.

Harnessing the Power of Email Marketing and Paid Advertising

Email marketing remains one of the most effective ways to nurture leads and drive sales. You'll learn how to build and segment your email list, craft persuasive email campaigns, and measure their success. In addition to organic strategies, paid advertising such as pay-per-click (PPC) campaigns can provide a significant boost to your online visibility. We'll explore the different types of paid advertising, how to set up and manage campaigns, and optimize your ad spend for maximum return on investment.

Embracing Innovation and Sustainability

The digital marketing landscape is constantly evolving, with new trends and technologies emerging at a rapid pace. We'll discuss the latest innovations, such as voice search, augmented reality (AR), and blockchain, and how they can be leveraged to enhance your marketing efforts. Moreover, sustainable marketing practices are becoming increasingly important as consumers prioritize ethical and environmentally friendly brands. This book will provide insights into creating a sustainable marketing plan that aligns with your values and resonates with your audience.

Conclusion

"Marketing Your Small Business Online in 2025" is more than just a guide; it's a roadmap to digital marketing success. By understanding your audience, building a strong online presence, leveraging the power of content and SEO, mastering social media and email marketing, and staying ahead of emerging trends, you'll be well-equipped to navigate the complexities of online marketing and drive your small business to new heights. Let this book be your companion on this exciting journey, empowering you to make informed decisions and achieve lasting success in the digital world.

Chapter 1:

Introduction to Online Marketing in 2025

The digital age has brought about a revolution in how

businesses operate and interact with their customers. Online marketing has become an indispensable tool for small businesses, providing them with the means to reach a global audience and compete with larger enterprises. In 2025, the landscape of online marketing is more dynamic and complex than ever before, with new technologies, platforms, and strategies continually emerging.

The Evolution of Online Marketing

Online marketing has come a long way since the early days of the internet. Initially, businesses relied on simple websites and email campaigns to reach their customers. However, with the advent of social media, mobile technology, and advanced analytics, the scope and capabilities of online marketing have expanded exponentially. Today, businesses can leverage a wide range of tools and techniques to engage with their audience, from social media advertising and influencer partnerships to search engine optimization and content marketing.

The Importance of Digital Presence

In the modern business landscape, having a strong digital presence is essential for success. Your online presence serves as the first point of contact between your business and potential customers. It encompasses your website, social media profiles, online reviews, and more. A well-designed and user-friendly website is the cornerstone of your digital presence, providing visitors with valuable information about your products or services and guiding them through the buyer's journey.

Key Components of Online Marketing

To effectively market your small business online, it's crucial to understand the key components of online marketing and how they work together to achieve your goals. These components include:

1. **Search Engine Optimization (SEO):** SEO involves optimizing your website and content to rank

higher in search engine results, making it easier for potential customers to find you online. This includes keyword research, on-page optimization, and building high-quality backlinks.

2. **Content Marketing:** Content marketing focuses on creating and distributing valuable, relevant, and consistent content to attract and engage your target audience. This can include

blog posts, articles, videos, infographics, and more.

3. **Social Media Marketing:** Social media platforms like Facebook, Instagram, Twitter, and LinkedIn provide businesses with opportunities to connect with their audience, share content, and build brand awareness. Effective social media marketing involves creating engaging content, interacting with followers,

and running targeted ad campaigns.

4. **Email Marketing:** Email marketing remains a powerful tool for nurturing leads and driving sales. By building a segmented email list and crafting personalized email campaigns, businesses can deliver targeted messages that resonate with their audience.

5. **Paid Advertising:** Paid advertising, such as pay-per-click (PPC) campaigns and social media ads, allows businesses to reach a larger audience and drive targeted traffic to their website. By setting a budget and targeting specific demographics, businesses can achieve measurable results.

Adapting to Changing Trends

The world of online marketing is constantly evolving, with new trends and technologies shaping the way businesses connect with their audience. In 2025, several key trends are expected to influence online marketing strategies:

1. **Artificial Intelligence (AI) and Machine Learning:** AI and machine learning are revolutionizing online marketing by enabling businesses to analyze vast

amounts of data and make data-driven decisions. These technologies can be used to personalize marketing messages, optimize ad campaigns, and predict customer behavior.

2. **Voice Search Optimization:** With the increasing popularity of voice-activated devices like Amazon Echo and Google Home, optimizing for voice search is becoming more

important. This involves creating content that answers common questions and uses natural language to improve search rankings.

3. **Video Marketing:** Video content continues to dominate online marketing, with platforms like YouTube, TikTok, and Instagram offering businesses new ways to engage with their audience. Creating high-quality video

content can help businesses build brand awareness and drive conversions.

4. **Sustainability and Ethical Marketing:** Consumers are increasingly prioritizing brands that align with their values and demonstrate a commitment to sustainability and ethical practices. Businesses that embrace these principles can build trust and loyalty with their audience.

Conclusion

As we navigate the complexities of online marketing in 2025, it's essential for small businesses to stay informed and adaptable. By understanding the key components of online marketing and embracing new trends and technologies, you can create a comprehensive and effective marketing strategy that drives growth and success. This book will serve as your guide, providing you with the knowledge and tools needed to thrive in the digital age. Whether you're just starting out or looking to refine your existing strategies, "Marketing Your Small Business Online in 2025" will empower you to make informed decisions and achieve your business goals.

Chapter 2:

Understanding Your Audience

In the realm of online marketing, understanding your audience is the cornerstone of success. Knowing who your customers are, what they need, and how they behave allows you to tailor your marketing efforts effectively, ensuring that your messages resonate and drive engagement. This chapter will delve into the essential aspects of understanding your audience, from conducting market research and creating buyer personas to analyzing customer data and leveraging insights for better marketing outcomes.

The Importance of Audience Research

Audience research is the process of gathering and analyzing information about your target customers. This includes demographic data, such as age, gender, location, and income level, as well as psychographic data, which covers interests, values, attitudes, and lifestyles. By understanding these aspects, you can create more targeted and relevant marketing campaigns that address the specific needs and preferences of your audience.

Conducting Market Research

Market research involves using various methods to collect data about your target audience. These methods can be broadly categorized into primary and secondary research.

1. **Primary Research:** Primary research involves collecting data directly from your target audience through surveys, interviews, focus groups, and observations. This type of research provides firsthand insights into customer behaviors,

preferences, and pain points.

2. **Secondary Research:** Secondary research involves analyzing existing data from sources such as industry reports, market studies, and competitor analysis. This type of research helps you understand broader market trends and benchmarks.

Creating Buyer Personas

Buyer personas are fictional representations of your ideal customers based on the data you have gathered. These personas help you visualize and understand your audience better, enabling you to create more personalized and effective marketing strategies. A detailed buyer persona includes:

- **Demographic Information:** Age, gender, income, education, occupation, and location.

- **Psychographic Information:** Interests, values, attitudes, and lifestyle.
- **Behavioral Information:** Purchasing behavior, brand loyalty, and online activity.
- **Pain Points and Challenges:** The problems and challenges your customers face that your product or service can solve.

- **Goals and Motivations:** What your customers aim to achieve and what motivates their purchasing decisions.

Analyzing Customer Data

Data analysis is a critical component of understanding your audience. By leveraging tools like Google Analytics, social media insights, and customer relationship management (CRM) systems, you can gain valuable insights into customer behavior and preferences. Key metrics to analyze include:

- **Website Traffic:** Understanding where your visitors come from, which pages they visit, and how long they stay on your site.
- **Conversion Rates:** Measuring the percentage of visitors who take a desired action, such as making a purchase or signing up for a newsletter.

- **Customer Engagement:** Analyzing interactions with your content, including likes, shares, comments, and click-through rates.
- **Sales Data:** Tracking sales trends, average order value, and customer lifetime value to identify patterns and opportunities for growth.

Leveraging Insights for Better Marketing

Once you have a clear understanding of your audience, you can leverage these insights to create more effective marketing strategies. This includes:

1. **Personalized Marketing:** Tailoring your messages and offers to meet the specific needs and preferences of different segments of your audience. Personalized marketing can significantly improve

engagement and
conversion rates.

2. **Targeted Advertising:**
   Using data to create
   targeted ad campaigns that
   reach the right people at
   the right time. This includes
   setting up audience
   segments based on
   demographics, interests,
   and behaviors.

3. **Content Creation:**
   Developing content that

resonates with your
audience, addresses their
pain points, and provides
value. This can include blog
posts, videos, social media
content, and more.

4. **Customer Experience:**
Enhancing the overall
customer experience by
understanding their journey
and identifying
opportunities to improve
touchpoints. This includes
optimizing your website,

streamlining the checkout process, and providing excellent customer support.

Conclusion

Understanding your audience is a fundamental aspect of successful online marketing. By conducting thorough market research, creating detailed buyer personas, analyzing customer data, and leveraging insights, you can create marketing strategies that are tailored to the needs and preferences of your target audience. This chapter has provided you with the tools and techniques needed to gain a deeper understanding of your customers, enabling you to connect with them on a more meaningful level and drive business growth. As you move forward, keep these principles in mind and continuously refine your approach based on new data and insights. This will ensure that your marketing efforts remain relevant and effective in the ever-changing digital landscape.

Chapter 3:

Building a Solid Online Presence

A strong online presence is essential for any small business looking to succeed in the digital age. Your online presence is your virtual storefront, representing your brand and serving as the first point of contact for many potential customers. In this chapter, we will explore the key elements of building a solid online presence, including creating a professional website, optimizing for search engines, maintaining a cohesive brand identity, and leveraging social media effectively.

Creating a Professional Website

Your website is the cornerstone of your online presence. It is where potential customers go to learn more about your products or services, make purchases, and engage with your brand. A professional website should be visually appealing, easy to navigate, and optimized for both desktop and mobile devices.

1. **Design and Layout:** Your website should have a clean and modern design that reflects your brand identity. Use consistent colors, fonts, and imagery to create a

cohesive look. The layout should be intuitive, with clear navigation menus and easy access to important information.

2. **Content:** High-quality content is essential for engaging visitors and providing value. This includes informative and persuasive copy, high-resolution images, and engaging videos. Make sure your content is well-

organized and easy to read, with clear headings and concise paragraphs.

3. **Functionality:** Your website should be fully functional, with fast loading times and no broken links. Ensure that all forms, buttons, and interactive elements work correctly. Additionally, make sure your website is mobile-friendly, as more and more users are accessing the

internet through their smartphones.

4. **Call to Action (CTA):** Every page on your website should have a clear and compelling call to action, guiding visitors towards the desired action, whether it's making a purchase, signing up for a newsletter, or contacting you for more information.

Search Engine Optimization (SEO)

SEO is crucial for improving your website's visibility in search engine results and driving organic traffic. By optimizing your website for search engines, you can increase your chances of being found by potential customers.

1. **Keyword Research:** Identify relevant keywords

and phrases that your target audience is likely to search for. Use tools like Google Keyword Planner, Ahrefs, or SEMrush to find keywords with high search volume and low competition.

2. **On-Page SEO:** Optimize your website's content and structure for search engines. This includes using target keywords in your titles, headings, and meta

descriptions, as well as
optimizing your URLs,
images, and internal links.

3. **Content Quality:** Create
   high-quality, valuable
   content that addresses the
   needs and interests of your
   audience. This can include
   blog posts, articles, guides,
   and FAQs. Regularly update
   your content to keep it
   fresh and relevant.

4. **Technical SEO:** Ensure that your website's technical aspects are optimized for search engines. This includes having a fast loading speed, a secure HTTPS connection, a mobile-friendly design, and a clear site structure with XML sitemaps.

Maintaining a Cohesive Brand Identity

Your brand identity is the visual and verbal representation of your business. It includes your logo, colors, fonts, tone of voice, and overall style. Maintaining a cohesive brand identity across all online channels is crucial for building brand recognition and trust.

1. **Brand Guidelines:** Develop a set of brand guidelines that outline the key elements of your brand identity. This includes your

logo, color palette, typography, imagery, and tone of voice. Ensure that all team members and external partners adhere to these guidelines.

2. **Consistency:** Apply your brand identity consistently across all online platforms, including your website, social media profiles, email campaigns, and online ads. This helps create a unified and professional

appearance that resonates with your audience.

3. **Authenticity:** Your brand identity should reflect the true values and personality of your business. Be authentic and transparent in your communications, and build genuine connections with your audience.

Leveraging Social Media Effectively

Social media platforms offer powerful opportunities for businesses to connect with their audience, share content, and build brand awareness. To leverage social media effectively, you need to choose the right platforms, create engaging content, and interact with your followers.

1. **Platform Selection:** Identify the social media platforms that are most popular with your target

audience. Common platforms include Facebook, Instagram, Twitter, LinkedIn, and Pinterest. Focus on the platforms that align with your business goals and audience demographics.

2. **Content Strategy:** Develop a content strategy that includes a mix of promotional, educational, and entertaining content. Use a variety of formats, such as images, videos,

stories, and live streams, to keep your audience engaged.

3. **Engagement:** Actively engage with your followers by responding to comments, messages, and mentions. Encourage user-generated content by running contests, asking questions, and sharing customer testimonials.

4. **Analytics:** Use social media analytics tools to track your performance and measure the effectiveness of your campaigns. Monitor key metrics such as reach, engagement, and conversion rates, and use this data to refine your strategy.

Conclusion

Building a solid online presence is essential for small businesses looking to succeed in the digital age. By creating a professional website, optimizing for search engines, maintaining a cohesive brand identity, and leveraging social media effectively, you can establish a strong and credible online presence that attracts and engages potential customers. As you implement these strategies, remember to stay adaptable and continuously refine your approach based on data and feedback. This will ensure that your online presence remains relevant and effective in the ever-changing digital landscape.

Chapter 4:

Content Marketing Strategies

Content marketing is a powerful tool for attracting, engaging, and retaining customers. By creating and distributing valuable, relevant content, you can establish your brand as an authority in your industry, build trust with your audience, and drive traffic and conversions. In this chapter, we will explore effective content marketing strategies, including developing a content plan, creating high-quality content, and distributing it across various channels.

Developing a Content Plan

A well-structured content plan is the foundation of successful content marketing. It helps you organize your efforts, ensure consistency, and align your content with your business goals.

1. **Set Goals:** Define clear and measurable goals for your content marketing efforts. These can include increasing website traffic, generating leads, improving brand awareness, or boosting customer engagement.

2. **Identify Your Audience:** Understand your target audience and their needs, preferences, and pain points. Use buyer personas

to guide your content creation and ensure that your content resonates with your audience.

3. **Content Themes:** Choose overarching themes that align with your business objectives and audience interests. These themes will guide your content creation and ensure that your content remains focused and relevant.

4. **Content Calendar:** Create a
   content calendar to plan
   and schedule your content.
   This helps you maintain a
   consistent posting schedule
   and ensures that your
   content is timely and
   relevant. Include important
   dates, such as holidays,
   industry events, and
   product launches.

Creating High-Quality Content

High-quality content is essential for attracting and retaining your audience. It should be informative, engaging, and valuable, addressing the needs and interests of your target audience.

1. **Blog Posts:** Blogging is a popular and effective content marketing strategy. Write informative and well-researched blog posts that provide value to your audience. Use engaging

headlines, subheadings, and visuals to enhance readability.

2. **Videos:** Video content is highly engaging and can help you connect with your audience on a deeper level. Create high-quality videos that showcase your products, share customer testimonials, provide tutorials, or offer behind-the-scenes insights.

3. **Infographics:** Infographics are visual representations of information that make complex data easy to understand. Use infographics to present statistics, processes, or comparisons in a visually appealing and digestible format.

4. **Ebooks and Guides:** Ebooks and guides are comprehensive resources that provide in-depth

information on a specific topic. Use these formats to demonstrate your expertise and provide valuable insights to your audience.

5. **Webinars and Podcasts:** Webinars and podcasts are interactive content formats that allow you to engage with your audience in real-time. Use these platforms to share expert knowledge, conduct interviews, or discuss industry trends.

Distributing Your Content

Creating high-quality content is only half the battle; you also need to distribute it effectively to reach your target audience. Use a mix of organic and paid distribution channels to maximize your content's reach and impact.

1. **Social Media:** Share your content on social media platforms to increase visibility and engagement.

Use relevant hashtags, tag influencers and partners, and encourage your followers to share your content.

2. **Email Marketing:** Use email marketing to distribute your content to your subscribers. Send newsletters, updates, and personalized recommendations to keep your audience informed and engaged.

3. **SEO:** Optimize your content for search engines to improve its visibility and drive organic traffic. Use relevant keywords, meta tags, and high-quality backlinks to boost your search engine rankings.

4. **Paid Advertising:** Use paid advertising, such as pay-per-click (PPC) campaigns and sponsored posts, to promote your content to a wider audience. Target

specific demographics and interests to ensure that your content reaches the right people.

5. **Collaborations and Guest Posting:** Collaborate with influencers, industry experts, and other businesses to expand your reach. Write guest posts for reputable blogs, participate in joint webinars, and share each other's content to tap into new audiences.

Measuring and Analyzing Your Content's Performance

To ensure that your content marketing efforts are effective, you need to measure and analyze your content's performance. Use analytics tools to track key metrics and gain insights into what works and what doesn't.

1. **Traffic:** Monitor the number of visitors to your website and the sources of

your traffic. Identify which content drives the most traffic and optimize your efforts accordingly.

2. **Engagement:** Track engagement metrics, such as likes, shares, comments, and time spent on your content. High engagement indicates that your content resonates with your audience.

3. **Conversions:** Measure the number of conversions generated by your content, such as leads, sales, or sign-ups. Identify which content is most effective at driving conversions and replicate its success.

4. **Return on Investment (ROI):** Calculate the ROI of your content marketing efforts by comparing the cost of creating and distributing your content

with the revenue generated. Use this data to make informed decisions about your content strategy.

Conclusion

Content marketing is a powerful strategy for attracting, engaging, and retaining customers. By developing a comprehensive content plan, creating high-quality content, distributing it effectively, and measuring its performance, you can build a strong and influential online presence. As you implement these strategies, remember to stay adaptable and continuously refine your approach based on data and feedback. This will ensure that your content marketing efforts remain relevant and effective in the ever-changing digital landscape.

Chapter 5:

Search Engine Optimization (SEO)

Search engine optimization (SEO) is a critical component of online marketing that involves optimizing your website and content to rank higher in search engine results. By improving your SEO, you can increase your website's visibility, drive organic traffic, and attract more potential customers. In this chapter, we will explore the essential elements of SEO, including keyword research, on-page optimization, technical SEO, and link building.

Keyword Research

Keyword research is the foundation of SEO. It involves identifying the keywords and phrases that your target audience is likely to search for. By understanding the search intent behind these keywords, you can create content that meets their needs and ranks well in search engine results.

1. **Identify Relevant Keywords:** Use keyword research tools like Google Keyword Planner, Ahrefs, or

SEMrush to find relevant keywords for your industry. Look for keywords with high search volume and low competition.

2. **Analyze Search Intent:** Understand the search intent behind each keyword. Are users looking for information, products, services, or solutions? Create content that addresses their specific

needs and provides
valuable information.

3. **Long-Tail Keywords:** Focus
   on long-tail keywords,
   which are more specific and
   less competitive than short-
   tail keywords. Long-tail
   keywords often have higher
   conversion rates because
   they target users with a
   clear intent.

4. **Keyword Grouping:** Group
   related keywords together

to create comprehensive content that covers a topic in-depth. This helps improve your content's relevance and authority.

On-Page Optimization

On-page optimization involves optimizing individual pages on your website to improve their search engine rankings. This includes optimizing content, meta tags, images, and internal links.

1. **Title Tags:** Use relevant keywords in your title tags to improve your page's visibility in search engine results. Keep your title tags concise, compelling, and within 60 characters.

2. **Meta Descriptions:** Write informative and persuasive meta descriptions that summarize your page's content. Use relevant keywords and keep your meta descriptions within 160 characters.

3. **Headings:** Use heading tags (H1, H2, H3) to structure your content and make it easy to read. Include relevant keywords

in your headings to improve their SEO value.

4. **Content Quality:** Create high-quality, valuable content that addresses the needs and interests of your audience. Use relevant keywords naturally and avoid keyword stuffing.

5. **Images:** Optimize your images by using descriptive file names, alt text, and captions. Compress your

images to improve your page's loading speed.

6. **Internal Links:** Use internal links to connect related pages on your website. This helps search engines understand your site's structure and improves user navigation.

Technical SEO

Technical SEO involves optimizing the technical aspects of your website to improve its search engine rankings. This includes site speed, mobile-friendliness, security, and site architecture.

1. **Site Speed:** Ensure that your website loads quickly by optimizing images, using a content delivery network (CDN), and minimizing HTTP requests. A fast-loading website provides a better user experience and improves your search engine rankings.

2. **Mobile-Friendliness:** Ensure that your website is mobile-friendly by using a responsive design. Google prioritizes mobile-friendly websites in its search results, so it's essential to provide a seamless experience for mobile users.

3. **Security:** Use HTTPS encryption to secure your website and protect user data. Google prioritizes secure websites in its search

results, so it's essential to have an SSL certificate.

4. **Site Architecture:** Ensure that your website has a clear and logical structure with easy navigation. Use a hierarchical structure with categories and subcategories, and create an XML sitemap to help search engines crawl your site.

Link Building

Link building is the process of acquiring high-quality backlinks from other websites to improve your site's authority and search engine rankings. Backlinks are one of the most important ranking factors for SEO.

1. **Create High-Quality Content:** Create valuable and shareable content that other websites want to link to. This includes blog posts, articles, infographics, videos, and guides.

2. **Guest Blogging:** Write guest posts for reputable blogs in your industry. This helps you build relationships with other websites and acquire high-quality backlinks.

3. **Outreach:** Reach out to other websites and influencers in your industry to request backlinks. Personalize your outreach messages and highlight the value of your content.

4. **Directory Submissions:** Submit your website to relevant online directories and industry-specific listings. This helps you acquire backlinks and improve your online visibility.

5. **Social Media:** Share your content on social media platforms to increase its visibility and attract backlinks. Engage with your

audience and encourage
them to share your content.

Conclusion

Search engine optimization
(SEO) is a critical component of
online marketing that involves
optimizing your website and
content to rank higher in search
engine results. By focusing on
keyword research, on-page
optimization, technical SEO, and
link building, you can improve
your website's visibility, drive

organic traffic, and attract more potential customers. As you implement these strategies, remember to stay up-to-date with the latest SEO trends and best practices, as search engine algorithms are constantly evolving. By continuously refining your approach and optimizing your efforts, you can achieve long-term success in the competitive digital landscape.

Chapter 6:

Social Media Marketing

Social media marketing is a powerful way for small businesses to reach their target audience, build brand awareness, and drive engagement. With billions of active users across various platforms, social media offers unparalleled opportunities for businesses to connect with their customers. In this chapter, we will explore effective social media marketing strategies, including choosing the right platforms, creating engaging content, managing social media accounts, and measuring success.

Choosing the Right Platforms

The first step in social media marketing is choosing the platforms that are most relevant to your target audience. Each platform has its unique features, demographics, and best practices, so it's essential to select the ones that align with your business goals.

1. **Facebook:** With over 2.8 billion monthly active users, Facebook is a versatile platform suitable for businesses of all sizes. It

offers robust advertising options, diverse content formats, and extensive audience targeting capabilities.

2. **Instagram:** Popular among younger audiences, Instagram focuses on visual content, such as photos, videos, and stories. It's an excellent platform for businesses in industries like fashion, beauty, food, and lifestyle.

3. **Twitter:** Known for its real-time updates and concise messaging, Twitter is ideal for businesses looking to engage with their audience through news, updates, and customer service.

4. **LinkedIn:** A professional networking platform, LinkedIn is best suited for B2B businesses, recruitment, and professional services. It offers opportunities for

thought leadership, industry insights, and networking.

5. **Pinterest:** A visual discovery platform, Pinterest is popular among users seeking inspiration and ideas. It's particularly effective for businesses in the home decor, fashion, food, and DIY niches.

6. **TikTok:** A rapidly growing platform with a young user base, TikTok focuses on

short-form videos. It's ideal for businesses looking to create viral content and engage with a younger demographic.

Creating Engaging Content

Content is the heart of social media marketing. To capture and retain your audience's attention, you need to create engaging, valuable, and shareable content.

1. **Visual Content:** High-quality images, videos, and graphics are essential for capturing attention. Use visually appealing content to showcase your products, share behind-the-scenes glimpses, and tell your brand's story.

2. **Stories:** Stories are short, ephemeral content that appears at the top of users' feeds. They are perfect for sharing quick updates,

promotions, and interactive content like polls and quizzes.

3. **Live Videos:** Live streaming allows you to connect with your audience in real-time. Use live videos for product launches, Q&A sessions, tutorials, and behind-the-scenes tours.

4. **User-Generated Content (UGC):** Encourage your customers to create and

share content related to your brand. UGC builds trust and authenticity and can be repurposed for your own social media channels.

5. **Educational Content:** Provide value to your audience by sharing informative and educational content. This can include how-to guides, tutorials, industry insights, and tips related to your products or services.

6. **Interactive Content:**
   Engage your audience with interactive content like polls, quizzes, contests, and challenges. This type of content encourages participation and fosters a sense of community.

Managing Social Media Accounts

Effective social media management involves consistent posting, active engagement, and monitoring your performance. Use these best practices to manage your social media accounts effectively.

1. **Content Calendar:** Plan and schedule your content in advance using a content calendar. This helps you maintain a consistent posting schedule and ensures that your content aligns with your marketing goals.

2. **Automation Tools:** Use social media management tools like Hootsuite, Buffer, or Sprout Social to schedule posts, monitor mentions, and analyze performance. Automation tools save time and streamline your social media efforts.

3. **Engagement:** Actively engage with your audience by responding to comments, messages, and mentions. Show

appreciation for positive feedback, address concerns, and foster a sense of community.

4. **Hashtags:** Use relevant hashtags to increase the visibility of your content. Research popular and trending hashtags in your industry and create branded hashtags to encourage user-generated content.

5. **Influencer Collaborations:** Partner with influencers in your industry to reach a broader audience. Influencers can help you promote your products, share authentic reviews, and create engaging content.

Measuring Success

To ensure the effectiveness of your social media marketing efforts, you need to measure and analyze your performance.

Use analytics tools to track key metrics and gain insights into what works and what doesn't.

1. **Reach:** Measure the number of people who see your content. A higher reach indicates that your content is being discovered by a larger audience.

2. **Engagement:** Track engagement metrics such as likes, comments, shares, and saves. High

engagement shows that your content resonates with your audience.

3. **Followers:** Monitor the growth of your follower count over time. A steady increase in followers indicates that your brand is gaining traction and attracting new audiences.

4. **Click-Through Rate (CTR):** Measure the number of clicks on your social media

links. A high CTR indicates that your content is driving traffic to your website or landing pages.

5. **Conversion Rate:** Track the number of conversions generated from your social media efforts, such as sales, sign-ups, or downloads. This metric helps you measure the ROI of your social media campaigns.

6. **Sentiment Analysis:**
   Analyze the sentiment of comments and mentions to understand how your audience feels about your brand. Positive sentiment indicates strong brand affinity, while negative sentiment highlights areas for improvement.

Conclusion

Social media marketing is a powerful tool for small businesses to connect with their audience, build brand awareness, and drive engagement. By choosing the right platforms, creating engaging content, managing your social media accounts effectively, and measuring your success, you can harness the full potential of social media to grow your business. As you implement these strategies, remember to stay adaptable and continuously refine your approach based on data and feedback. This will ensure that your social media marketing efforts remain relevant and effective in the ever-changing digital landscape.

Chapter 7:

Email Marketing

Email marketing remains one of the most effective and cost-efficient ways to nurture leads, drive sales, and build long-term relationships with your customers. With a high return on investment (ROI) and the ability to deliver personalized messages directly to your audience's inbox, email marketing is a crucial component of any online marketing strategy. In this chapter, we will explore the essential elements of email marketing, including building and segmenting your email list, crafting compelling email campaigns, and measuring the success of your efforts.

Building and Segmenting Your Email List

A high-quality email list is the foundation of successful email marketing. Focus on building a list of engaged and interested subscribers who are genuinely interested in your products or services.

1. **Lead Magnets:** Offer valuable incentives, such as ebooks, guides, discounts, or free trials, to encourage

visitors to subscribe to your email list. Ensure that your lead magnets are relevant and provide real value to your audience.

2. **Opt-In Forms:** Use opt-in forms on your website, blog, and landing pages to capture email addresses. Place these forms in strategic locations, such as pop-ups, sidebars, and the footer, to maximize visibility and conversions.

3. **Segmentation:** Segment your email list based on various criteria, such as demographics, behavior, purchase history, and engagement levels. Segmentation allows you to send targeted and personalized emails that resonate with specific groups of subscribers.

4. **Double Opt-In:** Implement a double opt-in process to ensure that subscribers

confirm their email address and consent to receive emails from you. This helps maintain a high-quality list and reduces the risk of spam complaints.

Crafting Compelling Email Campaigns

Creating compelling and engaging email campaigns is essential for capturing your audience's attention and driving action. Follow these best practices to craft effective email campaigns.

1. **Personalization:** Personalize your emails by addressing subscribers by their name and tailoring the content to their preferences and behavior. Personalization increases engagement and builds stronger connections with your audience.

2. **Subject Lines:** Write attention-grabbing subject lines that entice subscribers to open your emails. Keep them concise, relevant, and intriguing, and avoid using spammy language.

3. **Content:** Provide valuable and relevant content that addresses your subscribers' needs and interests. This can include informative articles, product updates, promotions, and exclusive

offers. Use a mix of text, images, and videos to keep your emails engaging.

4. **Call to Action (CTA):** Include clear and compelling calls to action that guide subscribers towards the desired action, such as making a purchase, signing up for an event, or downloading a resource. Use actionable language and make your CTAs stand out.

5. **Design:** Ensure that your emails are visually appealing and easy to read. Use a clean and responsive design that looks great on both desktop and mobile devices. Break up your content with headings, bullet points, and images to enhance readability.

6. **A/B Testing:** Conduct A/B testing to optimize your email campaigns. Test different elements, such as

subject lines, CTAs, images, and content, to identify what resonates best with your audience.

Measuring Success

To ensure the effectiveness of your email marketing efforts, you need to measure and analyze key metrics. Use email marketing analytics tools to track your performance and gain insights into what works and what doesn't.

1. **Open Rate:** Measure the percentage of subscribers who open your emails. A high open rate indicates that your subject lines and sender name are compelling and relevant.

2. **Click-Through Rate (CTR):** Track the percentage of subscribers who click on links within your emails. A high CTR indicates that your content and CTAs are engaging and persuasive.

3. **Conversion Rate:** Measure the percentage of subscribers who complete the desired action, such as making a purchase or signing up for an event. This metric helps you assess the effectiveness of your email campaigns in driving conversions.

4. **Bounce Rate:** Monitor the percentage of emails that are not delivered to subscribers' inboxes. A high

bounce rate may indicate issues with your email list quality or delivery practices.

5. **Unsubscribe Rate:** Track the percentage of subscribers who opt-out of your email list. While some unsubscribes are normal, a high unsubscribe rate may indicate that your content is not meeting subscribers' expectations.

6. **ROI:** Calculate the return on investment (ROI) of your email marketing campaigns by comparing the revenue generated with the cost of your email marketing efforts. This metric helps you determine the overall effectiveness and profitability of your email marketing strategy.

Conclusion

Email marketing is a powerful and cost-effective way to nurture leads, drive sales, and build long-term relationships with your customers. By building and segmenting your email list, crafting compelling email campaigns, and measuring your success, you can maximize the impact of your email marketing efforts. As you implement these strategies, remember to stay adaptable and continuously refine your approach based on data and feedback. This will ensure that your email marketing efforts remain relevant and effective in the ever-changing digital landscape.

Chapter 8:

Paid Advertising: PPC and More

Paid advertising, including pay-per-click (PPC) campaigns and other forms of digital advertising, is a powerful way to increase your online visibility, drive targeted traffic, and achieve measurable results. In this chapter, we will explore various types of paid advertising, including PPC, display ads, social media ads, and retargeting. We will also discuss best practices for creating effective ad campaigns and measuring their success.

Types of Paid Advertising

There are several types of paid advertising that businesses can use to reach their target audience. Each type has its unique benefits and best practices.

1. **Pay-Per-Click (PPC):** PPC advertising involves bidding on keywords and paying a fee each time someone clicks on your ad. Google Ads is the most popular PPC platform, allowing businesses to display ads on search engine results pages (SERPs) and partner websites.

2. **Display Ads:** Display ads are visual advertisements that appear on websites,

apps, and social media platforms. They can include images, videos, and interactive elements. Google Display Network and various social media platforms offer display ad options.

3. **Social Media Ads:** Social media advertising involves placing ads on platforms like Facebook, Instagram, Twitter, LinkedIn, and Pinterest. These ads can be

highly targeted based on demographics, interests, and behaviors.

4. **Retargeting Ads:** Retargeting ads are shown to users who have previously visited your website or interacted with your brand. These ads remind potential customers of your products or services and encourage them to return and convert.

5. **Native Ads:** Native ads are designed to blend seamlessly with the content of the platform on which they appear. They often take the form of sponsored articles or recommended content and are less intrusive than traditional ads.

6. **Video Ads:** Video advertising involves creating and promoting video content on platforms

like YouTube, Facebook, and Instagram. Video ads can be highly engaging and effective in capturing attention.

Creating Effective Ad Campaigns

To create effective ad campaigns that drive results, follow these best practices.

1. **Define Your Goals:** Clearly define your advertising goals, such as increasing

website traffic, generating leads, boosting sales, or building brand awareness. Your goals will guide your ad strategy and metrics for success.

2. **Audience Targeting:** Use audience targeting options to reach the right people with your ads. Target based on demographics, interests, behaviors, and location to ensure your ads are seen by your ideal customers.

3. **Compelling Ad Copy:**
Write compelling ad copy
that captures attention and
communicates your value
proposition. Use clear and
concise language, highlight
benefits, and include a
strong call to action.

4. **Visual Appeal:** Create
visually appealing ads that
stand out and attract
attention. Use high-quality
images and videos, and

ensure your design aligns with your brand identity.

5. **Landing Pages:** Ensure that your ads lead to relevant and optimized landing pages. Your landing page should provide a seamless user experience and encourage visitors to take the desired action.

6. **A/B Testing:** Conduct A/B testing to compare different ad variations and identify

what works best. Test elements such as headlines, ad copy, images, and CTAs to optimize your ads for better performance.

Measuring Success

To measure the success of your paid advertising campaigns, track key performance metrics and analyze your results.

1. **Click-Through Rate (CTR):** Measure the percentage of users who click on your ad.

A high CTR indicates that your ad is compelling and relevant to your audience.

2. **Conversion Rate:** Track the percentage of users who complete the desired action after clicking on your ad, such as making a purchase or filling out a form. This metric helps you assess the effectiveness of your landing page and ad copy.

3. **Cost Per Click (CPC):** Calculate the average cost you pay for each click on your ad. Monitoring your CPC helps you manage your budget and optimize your bidding strategy.

4. **Cost Per Conversion (CPA):** Measure the cost of acquiring a new customer or lead through your ad campaign. A low CPA indicates that your ads are

cost-effective and driving valuable conversions.

5. **Return on Ad Spend (ROAS):** Calculate the revenue generated from your ad campaign relative to the amount spent. A high ROAS indicates a profitable ad campaign.

6. **Impressions:** Track the number of times your ad is displayed. While impressions alone do not

indicate success, they help you understand your ad's reach and visibility.

Conclusion

Paid advertising is a powerful tool for increasing your online visibility, driving targeted traffic, and achieving measurable results. By understanding the various types of paid advertising, creating effective ad campaigns, and measuring their success, you can maximize the impact of your advertising efforts. As you implement these strategies, remember to stay adaptable and continuously refine your approach based on data and feedback. This will ensure that your paid advertising efforts remain relevant and effective in the ever-changing digital landscape.

Chapter 9:

Influencer Marketing

Influencer marketing leverages the reach and credibility of influential individuals to promote your products or services. By partnering with influencers who align with your brand, you can tap into their engaged audience, build trust, and drive conversions. In this chapter, we will explore the key aspects of influencer marketing, including identifying the right influencers, building partnerships, creating impactful campaigns, and measuring success.

Identifying the Right Influencers

Finding the right influencers is crucial for the success of your influencer marketing campaigns. Look for individuals who align with your brand values, have a genuine connection with their audience, and can authentically promote your products.

1. **Relevance:** Choose influencers who operate within your industry or niche. Their content should be relevant to your products or services, and their audience should match your target demographics.

2. **Engagement:** Evaluate the influencer's engagement rate by examining their likes, comments, shares, and overall interaction with their

audience. High engagement indicates a strong and active following.

3. **Authenticity:** Look for influencers who are genuine and authentic in their content. Authenticity builds trust and credibility, making their endorsements more effective.

4. **Reach:** Consider the influencer's reach, including their follower count and the

platforms they use. While larger influencers have broader reach, micro-influencers often have more engaged and loyal followers.

5. **Reputation:** Research the influencer's reputation and past collaborations. Ensure they have a positive image and a history of successful partnerships.

Building Partnerships

Building strong and mutually beneficial partnerships with influencers is essential for successful campaigns. Approach influencers with a clear value proposition and establish a collaborative relationship.

1. **Outreach:** Reach out to influencers with a

personalized and professional pitch. Highlight why you believe they are a good fit for your brand and how the partnership can benefit both parties.

2. **Collaboration:** Work closely with influencers to develop campaign ideas and content. Provide them with creative freedom while ensuring that the content aligns with your brand message.

3. **Compensation:** Offer fair compensation for the influencer's time and effort. This can include monetary payment, free products, or other incentives. Be transparent about your budget and expectations.

4. **Contracts:** Use contracts to outline the terms of the partnership, including deliverables, timelines, compensation, and usage rights. Contracts help

ensure that both parties are on the same page and protect your interests.

Creating Impactful Campaigns

To create impactful influencer marketing campaigns, focus on authenticity, creativity, and alignment with your brand goals.

1. **Content:** Collaborate with influencers to create high-quality and engaging content that resonates with

their audience. This can include product reviews, tutorials, unboxings, sponsored posts, and more.

2. **Storytelling:** Encourage influencers to tell a compelling story that highlights the benefits of your products or services. Authentic storytelling builds trust and makes the content more relatable.

3. **Hashtags and Mentions:** Use branded hashtags and mentions to increase the visibility of your campaign. Encourage influencers to incorporate these elements in their posts.

4. **Exclusive Offers:** Provide influencers with exclusive discount codes or offers for their followers. This creates a sense of urgency and incentivizes conversions.

5. **Cross-Promotion:** Cross-promote the influencer's content on your own social media channels and website. This amplifies the reach of the campaign and strengthens the partnership.

Measuring Success

To evaluate the effectiveness of your influencer marketing campaigns, track key performance metrics and analyze the results.

1. **Reach:** Measure the total reach of the campaign, including the number of followers exposed to the content across all platforms.

2. **Engagement:** Track engagement metrics such as likes, comments, shares, and saves. High engagement indicates that the content resonated with the audience.

3. **Website Traffic:** Monitor the increase in website traffic generated from the influencer's content. Use UTM parameters to track specific links and sources.

4. **Conversions:** Measure the number of conversions, such as sales, sign-ups, or downloads, attributed to the influencer campaign. Use unique discount codes or affiliate links to track conversions.

5. **ROI:** Calculate the return on investment (ROI) of your influencer marketing campaign by comparing the revenue generated with the total cost of the partnership. A high ROI indicates a successful campaign.

Conclusion

Influencer marketing is a powerful strategy for leveraging the reach and credibility of influential individuals to promote your products or services. By identifying the right influencers, building strong partnerships, creating impactful campaigns, and measuring success, you can effectively harness the power of influencer marketing to drive brand awareness, trust, and conversions. As you implement these strategies, remember to stay adaptable and continuously refine your approach based on data and feedback. This will ensure that your influencer marketing efforts remain relevant and effective in the ever-changing digital landscape.

Chapter 10:

Analytics and Metrics

Analytics and metrics are crucial for understanding the performance of your online marketing efforts and making data-driven decisions. By tracking and analyzing key performance indicators (KPIs), you can identify what works, what doesn't, and how to optimize your strategies for better results. In this chapter, we will explore essential analytics and metrics, tools for tracking them, and best practices for using data to improve your online marketing campaigns.

Key Performance Indicators (KPIs)

KPIs are measurable values that indicate how effectively you are achieving your business goals. Here are some essential KPIs to track for your online marketing efforts:

1. **Website Traffic:** Measure the number of visitors to

your website. This includes total visits, unique visitors, and page views. Understanding your traffic patterns helps you identify popular content and sources of traffic.

2. **Conversion Rate:** Track the percentage of visitors who complete a desired action, such as making a purchase, filling out a form, or signing up for a newsletter. A high conversion rate indicates

effective marketing and user experience.

3. **Bounce Rate:** Measure the percentage of visitors who leave your website after viewing only one page. A high bounce rate may indicate that your content or website design needs improvement.

4. **Average Session Duration:** Track the average amount of time visitors spend on

your website. Longer sessions typically indicate higher engagement and interest in your content.

5. **Customer Acquisition Cost (CAC):** Calculate the cost of acquiring a new customer by dividing your total marketing expenses by the number of new customers acquired. Lowering your CAC improves your marketing efficiency.

6. **Customer Lifetime Value (CLV):** Estimate the total revenue a customer generates over their lifetime. Increasing your CLV helps maximize the return on your marketing investment.

7. **Return on Investment (ROI):** Measure the profitability of your marketing campaigns by comparing the revenue generated with the total

cost of your efforts. A high ROI indicates a successful campaign.

Tools for Tracking Analytics

Several tools can help you track and analyze your online marketing performance. Here are some popular options:

1. **Google Analytics:** A powerful and versatile tool for tracking website traffic, user behavior, and conversions. Google

Analytics provides detailed insights into your audience, acquisition channels, and site performance.

2. **Google Search Console:** A free tool that helps you monitor and maintain your site's presence in Google search results. It provides insights into search performance, indexing status, and potential issues.

3. **Social Media Analytics:**
   Most social media platforms
   offer built-in analytics tools
   to track engagement, reach,
   and audience
   demographics. Examples
   include Facebook Insights,
   Instagram Insights, and
   Twitter Analytics.

4. **Email Marketing
   Analytics:** Email marketing
   platforms like Mailchimp,
   Constant Contact, and
   HubSpot provide detailed

analytics on open rates, click-through rates, and conversion rates.

5. **SEO Tools:** Tools like Ahrefs, SEMrush, and Moz help you track your search engine rankings, analyze backlinks, and conduct keyword research.

6. **Marketing Automation Platforms:** Platforms like HubSpot, Marketo, and Pardot offer comprehensive

analytics and reporting features for tracking the performance of your marketing campaigns across multiple channels.

Using Data to Improve Your Marketing Efforts

Collecting and analyzing data is only valuable if you use it to inform your marketing strategies. Here are some best practices for leveraging data to improve your online marketing efforts:

1. **Set Clear Goals:** Define specific, measurable, achievable, relevant, and time-bound (SMART) goals for your marketing campaigns. This helps you focus on key metrics and measure your success.

2. **Regular Reporting:** Create regular reports to track your performance and identify

trends. Use visualizations like charts and graphs to make the data more accessible and actionable.

3. **Identify Patterns:** Look for patterns and correlations in your data to understand what drives success. For example, you might notice that certain types of content generate more engagement or that specific traffic sources have higher conversion rates.

4. **A/B Testing:** Conduct A/B testing to compare different versions of your marketing materials and identify what works best. Test elements like headlines, images, CTAs, and landing pages to optimize your campaigns.

5. **Iterate and Optimize:** Use your insights to make data-driven decisions and continuously optimize your marketing efforts. Experiment with new

strategies, track their performance, and refine your approach based on the results.

6. **Attribution Modeling:** Use attribution modeling to understand how different marketing channels contribute to conversions. This helps you allocate your budget more effectively and maximize your ROI.

Conclusion

Analytics and metrics are essential for understanding the performance of your online marketing efforts and making data-driven decisions. By tracking key performance indicators, using the right tools, and leveraging data to improve your strategies, you can optimize your marketing campaigns for better results. As you implement these practices, remember to stay adaptable and continuously refine your approach based on data and feedback. This will ensure that your online marketing efforts remain relevant and effective in the ever-changing digital landscape.

Chapter 11:

Mobile Marketing

With the increasing use of smartphones and mobile devices, mobile marketing has become a crucial aspect of any comprehensive online marketing strategy. Mobile marketing involves reaching your audience through mobile-optimized content, apps, and advertising to engage users on their preferred devices. In this chapter, we will explore the key components of mobile marketing, including mobile-friendly website design, mobile apps, SMS marketing, and mobile advertising.

Mobile-Friendly Website Design

A mobile-friendly website is essential for providing a

seamless user experience and improving your search engine rankings. Ensure that your website is optimized for mobile devices with the following best practices:

1. **Responsive Design:** Use a responsive design that automatically adjusts to fit the screen size of any device. This ensures that your website looks great and functions well on

smartphones, tablets, and desktops.

2. **Fast Loading Speed:** Optimize your website for fast loading times, as mobile users expect quick access to information. Compress images, minify code, and use a content delivery network (CDN) to improve performance.

3. **Easy Navigation:** Simplify your website's navigation

for mobile users. Use clear and concise menus, large buttons, and a logical layout to make it easy for users to find what they need.

4. **Readable Text:** Ensure that your text is legible on small screens by using a readable font size and sufficient line spacing. Avoid using long paragraphs and break up your content with headings and bullet points.

5. **Touch-Friendly Elements:** Design your website with touch-friendly elements, such as large buttons and interactive elements that are easy to tap. Avoid using elements that require precise clicks or hover actions.

Mobile Apps

Mobile apps provide a direct and convenient way to engage with your audience. They offer unique features and functionality that can enhance the user experience and drive customer loyalty.

1. **App Development:** Consider developing a mobile app if it adds value to your customers and aligns with your business goals. Hire experienced developers or use app development platforms to create a high-quality app.

2. **App Store Optimization (ASO):** Optimize your app's listing in app stores to improve its visibility and attract more downloads. Use relevant keywords, write compelling descriptions, and include high-quality screenshots and videos.

3. **User Experience:** Focus on delivering a seamless and intuitive user experience within your app. Ensure that

the app is easy to navigate, visually appealing, and provides valuable features and content.

4. **Push Notifications:** Use push notifications to send timely and relevant messages to your app users. This can include promotions, updates, reminders, and personalized offers. Be mindful of frequency to avoid overwhelming users.

5. **In-App Engagement:**
   Encourage users to engage
   with your app through
   gamification, rewards, and
   interactive features. Track
   user behavior and
   preferences to deliver
   personalized content and
   experiences.

SMS Marketing

SMS marketing involves sending
promotional messages, alerts,
and updates directly to users'

mobile phones via text messages. It's a highly effective way to reach your audience with timely and relevant information.

1. **Opt-In List:** Build a list of subscribers who have opted in to receive SMS messages from your business. Use lead magnets, website forms, and in-store sign-ups to encourage opt-ins.

2. **Personalization:** Personalize your SMS

messages by addressing subscribers by name and tailoring the content to their preferences and behavior. Personalized messages are more likely to be read and acted upon.

3. **Clear and Concise:** Keep your SMS messages clear and concise, as text messages have a character limit. Get straight to the point and include a strong call to action.

4. **Timing:** Send SMS messages at appropriate times to maximize engagement. Avoid sending messages too early in the morning or late at night. Consider the timing of your offers and promotions to ensure relevance.

5. **Compliance:** Ensure that your SMS marketing efforts comply with regulations and guidelines, such as obtaining consent and

providing an easy opt-out option for subscribers.

Mobile Advertising

Mobile advertising involves placing ads on mobile websites, apps, and social media platforms to reach users on their mobile devices. It offers various formats and targeting options to maximize your ad's impact.

1. **Ad Formats:** Use mobile-friendly ad formats, such as banner ads, interstitial ads,

native ads, and video ads. Choose the format that best fits your campaign goals and audience preferences.

2. **Targeting:** Use advanced targeting options to reach the right audience with your mobile ads. Target based on demographics, interests, behaviors, location, and device type to ensure relevance.

3. **Creative Elements:** Design visually appealing and engaging ad creatives that capture users' attention. Use clear and concise messaging, strong visuals, and compelling calls to action.

4. **Landing Pages:** Ensure that your ad's landing page is optimized for mobile devices. Provide a seamless and relevant user

experience that encourages conversions.

5. **Analytics:** Track the performance of your mobile ads using analytics tools. Monitor key metrics such as impressions, clicks, CTR, conversions, and ROI to measure success and optimize your campaigns.

Conclusion

Mobile marketing is an essential component of any

comprehensive online marketing strategy. By optimizing your website for mobile devices, developing engaging mobile apps, leveraging SMS marketing, and creating effective mobile advertising campaigns, you can reach and engage your audience on their preferred devices. As you implement these strategies, remember to stay adaptable and continuously refine your approach based on data and feedback. This will ensure that your mobile marketing efforts remain relevant and effective in the ever-changing digital landscape.

Chapter 12:

Video Marketing

Video marketing is a powerful tool for capturing attention, engaging your audience, and driving conversions. With the rise of video consumption on platforms like YouTube, Facebook, Instagram, and TikTok, businesses have unparalleled opportunities to connect with their audience through compelling video content. In this chapter, we will explore the key aspects of video marketing, including creating high-quality videos, choosing the right platforms, optimizing video content, and measuring success.

Creating High-Quality Videos

Creating high-quality video content is essential for capturing your audience's attention and delivering your message effectively. Follow these best practices to produce engaging and professional videos.

1. **Storytelling:** Tell a compelling story that resonates with your audience. Focus on delivering value, whether it's through educational content, entertaining stories, or emotional connections. A strong

narrative keeps viewers engaged and invested.

2. **Production Quality:** Invest in good equipment and production techniques to ensure high-quality video and audio. This includes using a good camera, microphone, lighting, and editing software. High production quality reflects positively on your brand.

3. **Script and Planning:** Plan your video content in advance and write a clear and concise script. Outline the key points you want to cover and ensure that your messaging is consistent and on-brand.

4. **Length:** Keep your videos concise and to the point. While the ideal length can vary depending on the platform and content type, shorter videos (under 2

minutes) tend to perform better in capturing and retaining viewers' attention.

5. **Visual Appeal:** Use visually appealing elements, such as high-quality images, graphics, animations, and text overlays, to enhance your video's engagement. Ensure that your visuals align with your brand identity.

Choosing the Right Platforms

Choosing the right platforms for your video content is crucial for reaching your target audience and maximizing your impact. Consider the following popular platforms for video marketing:

1. **YouTube:** The world's largest video-sharing platform, YouTube is ideal for hosting and sharing long-form video content. It offers robust search and discovery features, making

it easy for users to find your videos.

2. **Facebook:** Facebook supports both short and long-form video content, including live streaming. Use Facebook to share engaging videos, promote events, and connect with your audience through comments and shares.

3. **Instagram:** Instagram is popular for short-form

video content, including stories, reels, and IGTV. It's a great platform for visually appealing and creative videos that capture quick attention.

4. **TikTok:** TikTok is known for its short, viral videos and is popular among younger audiences. Use TikTok to create fun and engaging videos that leverage trends and challenges.

5. **LinkedIn:** LinkedIn is ideal for professional and B2B video content, such as industry insights, thought leadership, and company updates. Use LinkedIn to share educational and informative videos with your professional network.

6. **Your Website:** Embed videos on your website to enhance user experience and provide valuable content. Use videos on

landing pages, product pages, and blog posts to engage visitors and drive conversions.

Optimizing Video Content

Optimizing your video content helps improve its visibility, engagement, and performance. Follow these best practices to optimize your videos for different platforms:

1. **SEO:** Optimize your video titles, descriptions, and tags

with relevant keywords to improve search visibility. Include a compelling thumbnail and a clear call to action (CTA) in your video description.

2. **Captions and Subtitles:** Use captions and subtitles to make your videos accessible to a wider audience, including those with hearing impairments and non-native speakers.

Captions also improve engagement and retention.

3. **Thumbnails:** Create eye-catching and relevant thumbnails that entice users to click on your videos. Thumbnails should accurately represent the video's content and include branding elements.

4. **Engagement:** Encourage viewers to like, comment, share, and subscribe.

Engaging with your audience through comments and responses fosters a sense of community and boosts your video's visibility.

5. **Analytics:** Use platform analytics to track the performance of your videos. Monitor key metrics such as views, watch time, engagement, and conversion rates to

understand what works and optimize your content.

Measuring Success

To measure the success of your video marketing efforts, track key performance metrics and analyze the results. Use the following metrics to evaluate your video's impact:

1. **Views:** Measure the number of times your video has been viewed. A high

view count indicates strong reach and visibility.

2. **Watch Time:** Track the total amount of time viewers spend watching your videos. Longer watch times indicate higher engagement and interest in your content.

3. **Engagement:** Monitor engagement metrics such as likes, comments, shares, and subscribes. High

engagement indicates that your content resonates with your audience.

4. **Click-Through Rate (CTR):** Measure the percentage of viewers who click on your video's CTA or associated links. A high CTR indicates effective messaging and strong interest.

5. **Conversion Rate:** Track the number of conversions, such as sales, sign-ups, or

downloads, attributed to your video content. Use unique tracking links or codes to measure conversions accurately.

6. **ROI:** Calculate the return on investment (ROI) of your video marketing efforts by comparing the revenue generated with the cost of production and promotion. A high ROI indicates a successful campaign.

Conclusion

Video marketing is a powerful tool for capturing attention, engaging your audience, and driving conversions. By creating high-quality videos, choosing the right platforms, optimizing your content, and measuring success, you can effectively harness the power of video marketing to grow your business. As you implement these strategies, remember to stay adaptable and continuously refine your approach based on data and feedback. This will ensure that your video marketing efforts remain relevant and effective in the ever-changing digital landscape.

Chapter 13:

Local SEO and Marketing

Local SEO and marketing are essential for small businesses aiming to attract customers within their geographic area. By optimizing your online presence for local search, you can increase visibility, drive more traffic to your website, and bring more customers to your physical location. In this chapter, we will delve into the critical components of local SEO and marketing, including optimizing your Google Business Profile listing, building local citations, creating localized content, leveraging online reviews, and engaging through social media.

Optimizing Your Google Business Profile Listing

Google Business Profile (GMB) is a free tool that allows you to

manage your online presence
across Google Search and Maps.
An optimized GMB listing is
crucial for local SEO success.

1. **Complete Your Profile:**
   Ensure your GMB profile is
   fully complete and up-to-
   date. This includes your
   business name, address,
   phone number, website,
   business hours, and
   categories. Adding high-
   quality images and a

compelling business description is also essential.

2. **Accurate Information:** Make sure your NAP (Name, Address, Phone number) information is consistent across all online platforms. Inconsistencies can confuse customers and negatively impact your search rankings.

3. **Categories and Attributes:** Choose the most relevant

categories for your business and add attributes that highlight special features or services, such as "wheelchair accessible" or "free Wi-Fi."

4. **Posts and Updates:** Use GMB posts to share updates, promotions, events, and news with your audience. Regularly updating your profile keeps your information current and engaging.

5. **Q&A and Messaging:**
   Monitor and respond to questions and messages from customers. Providing prompt and helpful responses builds trust and improves customer satisfaction.

Building Local Citations

Local citations are online mentions of your business's name, address, and phone number. They help improve your

local search visibility and
credibility.

1. **Online Directories:** Submit
   your business information
   to reputable online
   directories, such as Yelp,
   Yellow Pages, TripAdvisor,
   and industry-specific
   directories. Ensure that your
   information is accurate and
   consistent.

2. **Local Listings:** List your
   business on local websites,

such as city or community directories, chambers of commerce, and local business associations. These listings help you connect with local customers and improve your local SEO.

3. **NAP Consistency:** Ensure that your NAP information is consistent across all citations. Inconsistent information can confuse search engines and harm your local search rankings.

Creating Localized Content

Creating localized content helps you connect with your local audience and improve your local search rankings. Focus on topics and keywords relevant to your geographic area.

1. **Local Keywords:** Incorporate local keywords into your website content, including city names, neighborhoods, and landmarks. Use these

keywords in your titles, headings, meta descriptions, and body text.

2. **Blog Posts:** Write blog posts about local events, news, and topics of interest to your community. Highlight local partnerships, customer stories, and community involvement.

3. **Landing Pages:** Create localized landing pages for different locations or

services. These pages should include local keywords, unique content, and relevant information about each location.

4. **Local Guides:** Develop comprehensive local guides that provide valuable information to your audience. These can include city guides, neighborhood overviews, and recommendations for local attractions, restaurants, and

events. Such guides not only provide useful content but also help to establish your business as a local authority.

Leveraging Online Reviews

Online reviews are critical for local SEO and building trust with potential customers. Positive reviews can improve your search rankings and influence customers' decisions.

1. **Encourage Reviews:**
   Actively encourage satisfied customers to leave reviews on Google, Yelp, Facebook, and other relevant platforms. You can request reviews through follow-up emails, on your website, and in person.

2. **Respond to Reviews:**
   Monitor and respond to reviews regularly. Thank customers for positive reviews and address any

negative feedback professionally and constructively. Engaging with reviewers shows that you value customer feedback and are committed to providing excellent service.

3. **Showcase Reviews:** Highlight positive reviews on your website and social media profiles. Featuring testimonials builds

credibility and trust with potential customers.

4. **Review Management Tools:** Use review management tools to streamline the process of monitoring, collecting, and responding to reviews. These tools can help you stay on top of your online reputation.

Local Link Building

Building local backlinks from reputable websites in your community can boost your local SEO and drive targeted traffic to your website.

1. **Local Partnerships:** Partner with local businesses, organizations, and influencers to exchange links. Collaborate on content, events, and promotions to build mutually beneficial relationships.

2. **Sponsorships and Donations:** Sponsor local events, charities, and community organizations. Many will provide backlinks to your website in return for your support.

3. **Local Media:** Reach out to local newspapers, blogs, and online publications to feature your business in articles, interviews, and press releases. These

features often include backlinks to your website.

4. **Guest Blogging:** Write guest posts for local blogs and websites. Provide valuable content that appeals to their audience while including links back to your website.

Utilizing Social Media for Local Engagement

Social media platforms are excellent tools for engaging with your local community and promoting your business.

1. **Local Content:** Share content that is relevant to your local audience, such as updates on local events, news, and community activities. Highlight your involvement in local initiatives and partnerships.

2. **Geotargeting:** Use geotargeting features on social media platforms to

reach users in specific locations. Promote location-based offers and events to engage your local audience.

3. **Local Hashtags:** Use local hashtags to increase the visibility of your posts within your community. Research popular local hashtags and incorporate them into your social media strategy.

4. **Community Groups:** Join
   and participate in local
   community groups on
   platforms like Facebook and
   Nextdoor. Engage in
   discussions, share valuable
   content, and build
   relationships with
   community members.

Monitoring and Analyzing Local SEO Performance

Regularly monitoring and
analyzing your local SEO

performance helps you understand what's working and where you can improve.

1. **Google Business Profile Insights:** Use GMB insights to track how customers find your business, where they come from, and how they interact with your profile. Analyze metrics such as views, searches, and actions.

2. **Local SEO Tools:** Use local SEO tools like Moz Local,

BrightLocal, and Whitespark to track your local search rankings, citations, and reviews. These tools provide valuable insights and help you manage your local SEO efforts.

3. **Website Analytics:** Monitor your website analytics to track local traffic, user behavior, and conversions. Use tools like Google Analytics to understand the impact of your local SEO

efforts on your website performance.

4. **Review Analytics:** Analyze the sentiment and trends in your online reviews. Identify common themes in feedback and use this information to improve your products, services, and customer experience.

Conclusion

Local SEO and marketing are essential for attracting

customers within your geographic area and growing your small business. By optimizing your Google Business Profile listing, building local citations, creating localized content, leveraging online reviews, and engaging with your community through social media, you can enhance your local visibility and drive more traffic to your business. As you implement these strategies, remember to stay adaptable and continuously refine your approach based on data and feedback. This will ensure that your local SEO and marketing efforts remain relevant and effective in the ever-changing digital landscape

Chapter 14:

E-commerce Strategies

E-commerce presents tremendous opportunities for small businesses to reach a global audience, increase sales, and grow their brand. In this chapter, we will explore effective e-commerce strategies, including setting up an online store, optimizing product listings, improving the customer experience, and utilizing marketing tactics to drive traffic and conversions.

Setting Up an Online Store

The foundation of any successful e-commerce business is a well-designed online store. Follow these best practices to set up your online store for success:

1. **Choose the Right Platform:** Select an e-commerce platform that meets your needs and budget. Popular options include Shopify, WooCommerce, BigCommerce, and Magento. Ensure the platform is user-friendly, scalable, and offers essential features like

payment processing and inventory management.

2. **Professional Design:** Invest in a professional and visually appealing design for your online store. Use high-quality images, consistent branding, and an intuitive layout to create a positive shopping experience.

3. **Mobile Optimization:** Ensure that your online

store is mobile-friendly. With a significant portion of online shopping done on mobile devices, a responsive design is crucial for capturing mobile traffic and providing a seamless user experience.

4. **Secure Payment Gateway:** Offer secure and convenient payment options for your customers. Use trusted payment gateways like PayPal, Stripe, or Square to

process transactions and protect customer data.

Optimizing Product Listings

Optimized product listings are key to attracting and converting customers. Focus on the following elements to create compelling and effective product listings:

1. **High-Quality Images:** Use high-resolution images that showcase your products from multiple angles.

Include zoom functionality and lifestyle images to give customers a better understanding of the product.

2. **Detailed Descriptions:** Write detailed and informative product descriptions that highlight the features, benefits, and specifications of your products. Use clear and concise language, and

incorporate relevant keywords for SEO.

3. **Customer Reviews:** Display customer reviews and ratings on your product pages. Positive reviews build trust and credibility, while detailed feedback helps potential buyers make informed decisions.

4. **Pricing and Availability:** Clearly display the price of each product, including any

discounts or promotions. Indicate the availability and estimated delivery time to manage customer expectations.

5. **SEO Optimization:** Optimize your product listings for search engines by using relevant keywords in titles, descriptions, and meta tags. This helps improve your product's visibility in search results.

Improving the Customer Experience

A positive customer experience is crucial for driving sales and building customer loyalty. Implement the following strategies to enhance the customer experience on your online store:

1. **Easy Navigation:** Ensure that your online store is easy to navigate. Use clear categories, filters, and

search functionality to help customers find products quickly and easily.

2. **Fast Loading Speed:** Optimize your website's loading speed to provide a smooth and efficient shopping experience. Compress images, use a content delivery network (CDN), and minimize code to improve performance.

3. **User-Friendly Checkout:** Simplify the checkout process to reduce cart abandonment. Use a single-page checkout, offer guest checkout options, and provide multiple payment methods.

4. **Customer Support:** Offer excellent customer support through various channels, such as live chat, email, and phone. Provide a comprehensive FAQ section

and self-service resources to help customers find answers quickly.

5. **Personalization:** Use personalization techniques to enhance the shopping experience. Recommend products based on browsing history, offer personalized discounts, and send targeted email campaigns.

Utilizing Marketing Tactics

Effective marketing tactics are essential for driving traffic to your online store and converting visitors into customers. Implement the following strategies to boost your e-commerce sales:

1. **Email Marketing:** Use email marketing to nurture leads, engage customers, and drive repeat purchases. Send personalized emails, promotional offers, and

product recommendations to your subscribers.

2. **Social Media Marketing:** Leverage social media platforms to promote your products, engage with your audience, and drive traffic to your online store. Use a mix of organic content and paid advertising to reach a broader audience.

3. **Content Marketing:** Create valuable and informative

content that attracts and engages your target audience. Use blog posts, videos, guides, and infographics to showcase your products and provide helpful information.

4. **SEO and PPC:** Optimize your online store for search engines and use pay-per-click (PPC) advertising to drive targeted traffic. Conduct keyword research, optimize your site structure,

and run Google Ads campaigns to increase visibility.

5. **Influencer Marketing:** Partner with influencers in your industry to promote your products to their audience. Influencers can help you reach new customers, build brand credibility, and drive sales.

6. **Retargeting:** Use retargeting ads to re-

engage visitors who have shown interest in your products but haven't made a purchase. Retargeting helps remind potential customers of your products and encourages them to complete their purchase.

Analyzing E-commerce Performance

Regularly analyzing your e-commerce performance helps you understand what's working and where you can improve. Use the following metrics to evaluate your online store's success:

1. **Traffic and Conversion Rates:** Monitor the number of visitors to your online store and the percentage of visitors who make a purchase. Identify patterns and trends to understand what drives traffic and conversions.

2. **Average Order Value (AOV):** Calculate the average amount spent per order. Increase your AOV by offering upsells, cross-sells, and bundle deals.

3. **Customer Acquisition Cost (CAC):** Measure the cost of acquiring a new customer. Lower your CAC by optimizing your marketing campaigns and targeting high-intent audiences.

4. **Customer Lifetime Value (CLV):** Estimate the total revenue a customer generates over their lifetime. Focus on customer retention strategies to maximize your CLV.

5. **Cart Abandonment Rate:** Track the percentage of visitors who add items to their cart but do not complete the purchase. Implement strategies like email reminders, exit-intent

popups, and simplified checkout to reduce cart abandonment.

Conclusion

E-commerce presents tremendous opportunities for small businesses to reach a global audience and grow their brand. By setting up a professional online store, optimizing product listings, improving the customer experience, and utilizing effective marketing tactics, you can drive traffic and conversions. As you implement these strategies, remember to stay adaptable and continuously refine your approach based on data and feedback. This will ensure that your e-commerce efforts remain relevant and effective in the ever-changing digital landscape.

Chapter 15:

Customer Relationship Management (CRM)

Customer Relationship Management (CRM) involves managing interactions with your customers to build strong relationships, enhance customer satisfaction, and drive long-term loyalty. A robust CRM strategy helps you understand your customers better, personalize their experience, and improve your overall business performance. In this chapter, we will explore the key components of CRM, including choosing the right CRM software, collecting and analyzing customer data, and implementing strategies to enhance customer relationships.

Choosing the Right CRM Software

The right CRM software can significantly impact your ability to manage customer relationships effectively. Consider the following factors when choosing a CRM system:

1. **Features:** Look for CRM software that offers

essential features such as contact management, sales automation, marketing automation, customer support, and analytics. Ensure that the software meets your specific business needs.

2. **Ease of Use:** Choose a CRM system that is user-friendly and easy to navigate. A complicated system can hinder adoption and productivity. Opt for

software with an intuitive interface and comprehensive training resources.

3. **Scalability:** Ensure that the CRM software can scale with your business as it grows. It should accommodate an increasing number of contacts, users, and advanced features as your business expands.

4. **Integration:** Choose CRM software that integrates seamlessly with your existing tools and systems, such as email marketing platforms, e-commerce platforms, and social media tools. Integration enhances efficiency and data consistency.

5. **Customization:** Opt for a CRM system that allows for customization to suit your business processes and

workflows. Customizable fields, dashboards, and reports enable you to tailor the system to your specific needs.

6. **Support and Training:** Consider the level of customer suppt and training provided by the CRM vendor. Access to responsive support and comprehensive training materials is essential for

successful implementation and adoption.

Collecting and Analyzing Customer Data

Collecting and analyzing customer data is crucial for understanding your customers and delivering personalized experiences. Implement the following strategies to gather and utilize customer data effectively:

1. **Contact Information:** Collect basic contact information, such as name, email, phone number, and address. Use forms, surveys, and sign-ups to capture this information.

2. **Behavioral Data:** Track customer interactions with your website, emails, social media, and other touchpoints. Use analytics tools to gather data on page views, clicks,

purchases, and engagement.

3. **Purchase History:** Record customer purchase history, including products bought, frequency of purchases, and average order value. This data helps you understand customer preferences and buying patterns.

4. **Feedback and Reviews:** Collect customer feedback through surveys, reviews,

and direct interactions. Analyze feedback to identify common themes, areas for improvement, and opportunities for innovation.

5. **Segmentation:** Segment your customers based on demographics, behavior, purchase history, and preferences. Use segmentation to deliver targeted and relevant marketing messages.

6. **Data Analysis:** Use CRM analytics tools to analyze customer data and gain insights into customer behavior, trends, and patterns. Leverage these insights to make data-driven decisions and optimize your marketing strategies.

Implementing CRM Strategies

Implementing effective CRM strategies helps you build strong customer relationships and drive long-term loyalty. Focus on the following strategies to enhance your CRM efforts:

1. **Personalization:** Use customer data to personalize your interactions and communications. Address customers by name, tailor recommendations based on their preferences, and send personalized offers and content.

2. **Customer Journey Mapping:** Create customer journey maps to visualize the entire customer experience from awareness to post-purchase. Identify key touchpoints and opportunities to enhance the customer journey.

3. **Automated Workflows:** Implement automated workflows to streamline repetitive tasks and improve efficiency. Use automation

for tasks like email campaigns, follow-ups, lead nurturing, and customer support.

4. **Customer Support:** Provide exceptional customer support through various channels, such as live chat, email, phone, and social media. Use your CRM system to track support tickets, responses, and resolutions.

5. **Loyalty Programs:** Develop loyalty programs to reward repeat customers and encourage long-term loyalty. Offer incentives such as discounts, exclusive offers, and early access to new products.

6. **Feedback and Improvement:** Regularly seek customer feedback and use it to improve your products, services, and processes. Show customers

that you value their input by implementing their suggestions and keeping them informed of changes.

Measuring CRM Success

To measure the success of your CRM efforts, track key performance metrics and analyze the results. Use the following metrics to evaluate your CRM performance:

1. **Customer Retention Rate:** Measure the percentage of

customers who continue to do business with you over a specific period. A high retention rate indicates strong customer loyalty and satisfaction.

2. **Customer Lifetime Value (CLV):** Calculate the total revenue a customer generates over their lifetime. Increasing CLV indicates successful CRM strategies that drive repeat

purchases and long-term loyalty.

3. **Customer Satisfaction (CSAT):** Use customer satisfaction surveys to gauge how satisfied customers are with your products, services, and overall experience. High CSAT scores reflect positive customer experiences.

4. **Net Promoter Score (NPS):** Measure the

likelihood of customers recommending your business to others. A high NPS indicates strong customer loyalty and positive word-of-mouth.

5. **Response Time:** Track the average time it takes to respond to customer inquiries and support tickets. Quick response times enhance customer satisfaction and trust.

6. **Sales Growth:** Monitor sales growth and revenue generated from your CRM efforts. Increased sales and revenue indicate successful CRM strategies that drive business growth.

Conclusion

Customer Relationship Management (CRM) is essential for building strong customer relationships, enhancing satisfaction, and driving long-term loyalty. By choosing the right CRM software, collecting and analyzing customer data, and implementing effective CRM strategies, you can optimize your interactions with customers and improve your overall business performance. As you implement these strategies, remember to stay adaptable and continuously refine your approach based on data and feedback. This will ensure that your CRM efforts remain

relevant and effective in the
ever-changing digital landscape.

Chapter 16:

Emerging Trends and Technologies

The digital marketing landscape is constantly evolving, with new trends and technologies shaping the way businesses connect with their audience. Staying ahead of these trends is essential for maintaining a competitive edge and effectively engaging your customers. In this chapter, we will explore emerging trends and technologies in online marketing, including artificial intelligence (AI), voice search optimization, augmented reality (AR), blockchain, and more.

Artificial Intelligence (AI)

Artificial intelligence is transforming digital marketing by enabling businesses to analyze vast amounts of data, automate tasks, and deliver personalized experiences. Here are some ways AI is being used in online marketing:

1. **Chatbots:** AI-powered chatbots provide instant customer support and engagement. They can

answer common questions, guide users through the purchasing process, and provide personalized recommendations.

2. **Predictive Analytics:** AI algorithms analyze customer data to predict future behavior and trends. Predictive analytics helps businesses make data-driven decisions and optimize marketing strategies.

3. **Personalization:** AI enables hyper-personalization by analyzing user behavior and preferences. Businesses can deliver personalized content, product recommendations, and offers based on individual user profiles.

4. **Content Creation:** AI tools like GPT-3 can generate high-quality content, such as blog posts, social media updates, and email

campaigns. These tools help marketers save time and maintain consistency.

5. **Ad Optimization:** AI algorithms optimize ad campaigns by analyzing performance data and adjusting bids, targeting, and creatives in real-time. This improves ad efficiency and ROI.

Voice Search Optimization

With the increasing use of voice-activated devices like Amazon Echo and Google Home, optimizing for voice search is becoming more important. Here are some strategies for voice search optimization:

1. **Natural Language:** Optimize your content for natural language queries. Voice searches tend to be longer and more conversational, so use long-

tail keywords and natural phrases in your content.

2. **Featured Snippets:** Aim to appear in featured snippets, as these are often read aloud by voice assistants. Provide concise and informative answers to common questions in your content.

3. **Local SEO:** Voice searches are often location-based, so ensure your local SEO is

strong. Optimize your Google Business Profile listing, use local keywords, and provide clear NAP information.

4. **FAQ Pages:** Create FAQ pages that address common questions related to your products or services. Use natural language and structure your content to provide clear and direct answers.

Augmented Reality (AR)

Augmented reality is enhancing the customer experience by providing interactive and immersive ways to explore products and services. Here are some applications of AR in digital marketing:

1. **Virtual Try-Ons:** AR allows customers to virtually try on products, such as clothing, accessories, and makeup, before making a purchase.

This enhances the shopping experience and reduces returns.

2. **Product Visualization:** AR enables customers to visualize how products will look in their environment. For example, furniture retailers can use AR to show how a piece will fit in a customer's home.

3. **Interactive Packaging:** AR can be used to create

interactive packaging experiences. Customers can scan product packaging to access additional content, such as tutorials, games, and promotions.

4. **AR Ads:** AR ads provide an engaging and interactive way to showcase products. These ads allow users to interact with products in a virtual environment, increasing engagement and conversion rates.

Blockchain Technology

Blockchain technology is revolutionizing digital marketing by providing greater transparency, security, and efficiency. Here are some ways blockchain is being used in online marketing:

1. **Transparent Advertising:** Blockchain enables transparent ad transactions by providing a decentralized ledger of all

ad interactions. This reduces fraud and ensures that advertisers get what they pay for.

2. **Data Privacy:** Blockchain allows users to control their personal data and grant access to marketers in a secure and transparent way. This enhances data privacy and builds trust with customers.

3. **Loyalty Programs:**
   Blockchain can streamline
   loyalty programs by
   providing a secure and
   transparent way to track
   and redeem rewards. This
   improves the customer
   experience and reduces
   fraud.

4. **Smart Contracts:** Smart
   contracts automate and
   enforce the terms of
   agreements between
   parties. In digital marketing,

smart contracts can automate ad placements, payments, and performance tracking.

Other Emerging Trends

In addition to AI, voice search, AR, and blockchain, several other emerging trends are shaping the future of digital marketing:

1. **Interactive Content:** Interactive content, such as quizzes, polls, and

interactive videos, engages users and provides a personalized experience. This type of content encourages participation and boosts engagement.

2. **Video Marketing:** Video content continues to dominate digital marketing. Live streaming, short-form videos, and personalized video messages are becoming increasingly

popular for engaging audiences.

3. **Social Commerce:** Social media platforms are integrating e-commerce features, allowing users to shop directly from their feeds. Social commerce streamlines the shopping experience and boosts conversions.

4. **Sustainability Marketing:** Consumers are increasingly

prioritizing brands that demonstrate a commitment to sustainability and ethical practices. Businesses are incorporating sustainability into their marketing strategies to attract conscious consumers.

Conclusion

Emerging trends and technologies are continually reshaping the digital marketing landscape. By staying informed and adapting to these changes, businesses can maintain a competitive edge and effectively engage their audience. As you explore these trends, remember to stay adaptable and continuously refine your approach based on data and feedback. This will ensure that your digital marketing efforts remain relevant and effective in the ever-changing digital landscape.

Chapter 17:

Creating a Sustainable Marketing Plan

A sustainable marketing plan is essential for the long-term

success of your small business. It involves developing strategies that are not only effective but also adaptable to changing market conditions and aligned with your business goals. In this chapter, we will explore the key components of a sustainable marketing plan, including setting clear objectives, defining your target audience, choosing the right marketing channels, and measuring your success.

Setting Clear Objectives

Clear and measurable objectives provide direction and focus for your marketing efforts. Follow these steps to set effective marketing objectives:

1. **Specific:** Define specific goals that clearly outline what you want to achieve. Avoid vague objectives and focus on concrete outcomes.

2. **Measurable:** Ensure that your objectives are

measurable so that you can track progress and assess success. Use metrics such as sales, leads, website traffic, and engagement.

3. **Achievable:** Set realistic goals that are attainable based on your resources and capabilities. Consider your current position and the challenges you may face.

4. **Relevant:** Align your marketing objectives with your overall business goals. Ensure that your marketing efforts support your broader strategic priorities.

5. **Time-Bound:** Establish a timeline for achieving your objectives. Set deadlines and milestones to keep your efforts on track and maintain momentum.

Defining Your Target Audience

Understanding your target audience is crucial for creating effective marketing strategies. Follow these steps to define your target audience:

1. **Market Research:** Conduct market research to gather data on your potential customers. Use surveys, focus groups, and analytics tools to gain insights into

their demographics, behaviors, and preferences.

2. **Buyer Personas:** Create detailed buyer personas that represent your ideal customers. Include information such as age, gender, income, interests, pain points, and buying behavior.

3. **Segmentation:** Segment your audience based on common characteristics and

needs. Use segmentation to deliver targeted and personalized marketing messages to different groups.

4. **Customer Journey:** Map out the customer journey to understand the key touchpoints and decision-making processes. Identify opportunities to engage and influence customers at each stage.

Choosing the Right Marketing Channels

Selecting the right marketing channels is essential for reaching your target audience and achieving your objectives. Consider the following factors when choosing marketing channels:

1. **Audience Preferences:** Choose channels that align with your audience's preferences and behaviors.

Consider where your target audience spends their time and how they consume content.

2. **Channel Strengths:** Evaluate the strengths and weaknesses of each marketing channel. Consider factors such as reach, engagement, cost, and effectiveness.

3. **Integrated Approach:** Use an integrated marketing

approach that combines multiple channels to maximize your reach and impact. Ensure that your messaging is consistent across all channels.

4. **Budget Allocation:** Allocate your marketing budget based on the potential ROI of each channel. Invest in channels that offer the highest return on investment and align with your objectives.

Measuring Success

Measuring the success of your marketing efforts is crucial for understanding what works and where you can improve. Follow these steps to measure your success:

1. **Key Metrics:** Identify key performance metrics that align with your objectives. Common metrics include website traffic, conversion rates, customer acquisition

cost, and customer lifetime value.

2. **Data Collection:** Use analytics tools to collect data on your marketing performance. Track metrics across different channels and campaigns to gain a comprehensive view of your results.

3. **Analysis:** Analyze your data to identify trends, patterns, and insights. Use this

information to understand what drives success and where you need to make adjustments.

4. **Reporting:** Create regular reports to track your progress and communicate your results to stakeholders. Use visualizations such as charts and graphs to make your data more accessible and actionable.

5. **Continuous Improvement:** Use your insights to continuously refine and optimize your marketing strategies. Experiment with new approaches, test different tactics, and iterate based on feedback and data.

Conclusion

Creating a sustainable marketing plan is essential for the long-term success of your small business. By setting clear objectives, defining your target audience, choosing the right marketing channels, and measuring your success, you can develop strategies that are effective and adaptable to changing market conditions. As you implement these strategies, remember to stay adaptable and continuously refine your approach based on data and feedback. This will ensure that your marketing efforts remain relevant and effective in the ever-changing digital landscape.

Type the following into your AI writer...

Please create a one month
social media content plan
for **BUSINESS NAME**.

They provide **SERVICE/PRODUCT** to the **GEOGRAPHIC** area. Create it as a Table and include some post about little known facts about **SERVICE/PRODUCT** and some puns related to **SERVICE/PRODUCT**, some reasons to contact **BUSINESS NAME**, and a call to action at least once per week.